BaBy HiP-HOP ™
AnD HOMeless
Mrs. Katie

Written By Danell L Stevens Sr.

This **Baby Hip Hop**
book belongs to....

_____

The Author
Danell L Stevens Sr.

I dedicate this inspirational children book to all humanity. I would also like to give a thanks to my kids Hamp, Dantrell, Bria, Kameeka, Little Danell and DJ for giving me the opportunity to observe there interest in Rap music when they where little kids. As I observed there interest in hip hop, I instantly noticed that I could possibly teach my children through Hip-Hop Rap Music.

I started testing this notion on my own kids, by educating them through rap music and I achieved outstanding results. Now you have this ethical story of a character who solves everyday problems. I now present to you the Baby Hip-Hop educational series Book Number 2.

ISBN 0-615-24538-6

Library of Congress Cataloging-in-Publication is available
Printed in the U.S.A.
Shot Entertainment Publishing Inc.
Fairfield, CA

Baby Hip-Hop
And Homeless
Mrs. Katie

Written By Danell Stevens Sr.

Illustrated By Solomon Perry

One day, Miss Hip-Hop was in the kitchen making supper while Little B was in his room playing his favorite Playstation game. The doorbell rang and Little B ran to the door and looked through the peephole. "It's Joe and Dooney, Mom."

"Okay, you can let them in." she replied. Little B opened the door with excitement, "What's up Joe, what's up Dooney?"

"Can you come out and play?" said Dooney. "You know today is our big basketball game."

"Okay, let me go and ask my mom if I can go." Little B ran to the kitchen and his mother instantly knew Little B was getting ready to ask for something.

"What do you want, B?" his mother asked as she busily prepare dinner.

"I wanted to know if I can go play basketball with Joe and Dooney at the park. It's our big game today."

"Just be back here before supper."

she said with a pleasant smile.

"Okay, bye!" Little B said as he dashed for the door.

"Be careful," Miss Hip Hop yelled with a reminder "And watch for the cars."

"I know, Mom," he assured while closing the door. "Okay guys, let's go and have some fun!"

They all headed towards the park while admiring the warm sunny day. The neighbors were full of joy and other kids were out having a good time enjoying the sunshine as well. Then Little B and his friends noticed a strange sight as they were entering the park . They saw a little old lady digging in a big green garbage can. She was pulling things out of the garbage and putting it in a shopping cart as if she was in a grocery store. "Hey guys, do you see what I see?" Little B whispered.

"Yeah, we see her," Joe whispered back. "What's wrong with her? It looks like she's looking for something to eat." said Dooney. Little B looked at Dooney and Joe and shook his head, "You know this isn't cool. We have to do something to help that old lady."

"But how are we going to help her?" asked Dooney, "Just look at her hair and those mismatched shoes she's wearing…and those jeans she has on; they have really big holes in them."

"Okay fellows, that's enough! We have to go into Operation Save the Old Lady. Is everybody ready?" yelled Little B. "Yes sir!" Joe and Dooney responded with a salute. "Okay, men, we are going to plan the rescue and do this in a kind and effective way." Little B commanded, sounding like a drill sergeant. "Yes sir!" Dooney and Joe responded.

"Let's check out our ammunition. Dooney?"

"I have one candy bar, sir."

"And what about you, Sergeant Joe?"

"I have one broken cookie in my back pocket, sir."

"Okay boys, let's go and help the old lady." Little B said, taking a few steps forward.

"I'm not supposed to talk to strangers!" Dooney cried in shock.

"Yeah, I can get in trouble for this." Joe said. "No you're not!" Little B protested, "My mother and father told me the same thing but they didn't say we couldn't help an old lady that is eating out of a garbage can like some animal. Let's go talk to her and see if we can be of some help. It's just not right for her to be eating out a garbage can."

The boys ran over to the old lady, "Excuse me, lady, why are you eating out of a garbage can?" they asked politely. The old lady replied in a low grumbling voice,

"I'm hungry. I don't have anything to eat and I don't have a home."

"No home?" the boys cried out at the same time in shock.

"That's right, no home." She said, and then went back to digging in the trashcan.

"So you mean to tell me that you

don't have a home or a family?" Little B exclaimed.

"I lost my home in a storm and I had a daughter but she ran off with some man and I haven't seen her for five years." The old lady answered sadly. "I'm sorry to hear that." Joe responded, his voice sounding as if he was going to cry. "Don't cry, child, everything will be okay. My name is Miss Katie. What are your names?"

"My name is Little B and these are my friends, Joe and Dooney." Little B looked at Joe and Dooney and they all began to reach in their pockets.

Joe pulled out a cookie, Dooney pulled out a candy bar and Little B pulled out a taffy stick then they each gave the treats to the old lady.

The lady looked up with a big smile on her face, "Oh, bless your little hearts…bless your hearts."

Miss Katie accepted the food, thanked them and put it in a container in her shopping basket.

She started pushing the basket and headed off on her way. Little B ran after her, "Where are you going?" he asked.

"I usually rest by the old bus station on First Street." She told him. "I will see you kids again. Thank you for your help."

"Okay, Miss Katie, you take care of yourself." Little B said warmly and ran back to where Joe and Dooney were standing. "You guys, this old lady needs major help and we have to come up with a plan." He told them seriously.

"But what about our basketball game?" asked Dooney. "This is more important than some basketball game; we have to help Miss Katie."

"What can we do?" Dooney said reluctantly, "We are just kids."

"But we are not just any kids!" Little B exclaimed, "We are smart kids. This is what we are going to do: we're going to ask our parents for some old clothes and sleeping bags and we can ask for seconds at dinner, too.

Then we'll put the food in a doggy bag and give it all to Miss Katie."

They all ran home to begin with their part of the plan. "Hey, Mom I'm home." Little B said as he walked into the house. "Hello. Go wash your hands and get ready for supper."

"Okay, Mom." Little B ran into the bathroom and washed his hands. When he came out, his father was giving Mrs Hip Hop a hug. "What's up, dad?" He said cheerfully. "Hey son, how was your day?"

"It was very interesting. Me and the boys were hanging out." Little B and his father sat down at the table.

Mrs. Hip Hop served the food then she sat down with Little B and his Father and they began to eat.

"Can I ask you a question, Mom?' said Little B, after a moment of thought.

"Yes, Baby, you can ask me anything you want."

"If you could help someone who has problems, would you help them?"

"It depends on what it is. Why?"

"I can't tell you right now, Mom, because it's top secret. If I tell you then I would be telling someone's secret." Little B started to eat his dinner and Mr. and Mrs Hip Hop started to talk about some bills that needed to be paid.

Little B interrupted their conversation, "Sorry Mom and Dad, Mom I am finished eating and I'm still hungry. Can I get some more food?"
"Sure B, just go get it yourself.
I'm talking to your father." She answered. Little B went into the kitchen and grabbed a plastic container. He filled it with fried chicken and beans and he also put some on his own plate then he hid the plastic container inside of the refrigerator.

Afterwards, he went back to the dinner table and finished his meal. When he was finished he said, "Mom, do you have any old clothes that you don't want? Me and the boys are working on something."

"What would you guys want with my old clothes, Little B?"

"Mom, this is top-secret. I can't tell you yet." He told her seriously.

"Okay, go look in the red box in the attic. That's where I put clothes that I don't need anymore."

"You're the best and nothing like the rest!" he exclaimed.

"Get out of here boy, you're so funny." She laughed and playfully pinched his cheek. He laughed too, "Thanks, Mom."

Smiling with anticipation, Little B went up the stairs to the attic and located the place where his Mother kept her old clothes. He put everything from the red box into a plastic bag before he went to bed.

The next day, Little B took the container of food and the bag of clothing to Joe's house.

"I have a whole bag of clothing and a container full of food for Miss Katie."

He told him, showing him the things he'd collected.

"Cool, I have some stuff too!" Joe said excitedly and ran to his room.

He came back with a bag of food and some old shoes that his mother had given him. Little B and Joe hoisted the bags and walked over to Dooney's house.

He was helping his dad wash the car but when he saw Little B and Joe he said, "Hey Dad, I have to go. My friends are coming and we have a mission to complete."

"Okay," his Dad said surprised, "But be back before it gets dark." Dooney ran into the house and grabbed his backpack then met Little B and Joe at the corner. "I have some food for Miss Katie. My parents gave me some canned food and a can opener."

"Now we can go find Miss Katie." Little B said with excitement.

They started walking to First Street to find Miss Katie. When they got there, they looked around. "I wonder where she is. She told us she would be around here." Little B commented. Dooney shrugged, "Maybe she meant the other bus bench."

The boys headed out to the next bus bench. "There she is." said Joe, pointing. "Come on you guys," said Little B.

When they walked up to where she was sitting, she looked up and smiled in surprise. "Hello, Miss Katie…we've been looking for you. We brought you some clothes and enough food for a few days." Little B told her humbly.

"Why, thank you boys. You all are so kind…I don't know how to repay you." She said in awe as the boys handed her the bags and containers.

"Miss Katie, you don't have to repay us…we get it free anyway." said Dooney. "My real name is Katie Smith and what are your names again?"

Little B answered, "My name is Baby Hip Hop and my friends are Joe Johnson and Dooney Jackson."

"Are you kin to Michael Jackson?" Miss Katie joked and they all laughed, "No Ma'am, I just have his last name but people ask me that all the time."

"Miss Katie, I made a rap song for you. Do you want to hear it?' asked Little B. "Yes son, I'd love to." She smiled.

"Okay, here goes…" He took a deep breath as Dooney made the sounds of the beat:

"There are some people out there
that really care
there some people out there
that just ain't fair
there some people out there
that just don't care
but me and Dooney
and my boy young Joe
we are here to tell you and let
everybody know
that life is precious
Use your brain as a weapon
'Cuz what the world needs is
a little bit of love
what the world needs is
more people to love.
What the world needs is
a little bit of love
what the world needs is
more people to love."

Then Joe took over and finished the rap as Dooney beat-boxed:

My mama said, 'son please don't cry'
just listen to your father,
everything is all right
They say go to school to get your
education
don't nothing come fast
you got to have some patience!

Miss Katie started clapping with a big smile on her face, "Where did you boys learn how to rap so well?"

"My Daddy is a rapper and I learned a lot from him." said Little B. "Joe and Dooney are in my group. We're called the Hip Hop Block."

"Well, young man, I think you all are going to make it to the top! Keep up the good work."

"Thank you Miss Katie." Little B said humbly. "Do you ever get scared out here all alone? There are a lot of evil people around."

"Sure, I do. If I didn't I wouldn't be human. I also get lonely out here. I just sit here and watch the cars go by all day."

"Do you get scared at night? What do you do when it rains?" Joe asked sadly. "Well, I just walk down that street to that overpass over there. I get right under it and I put on all the clothing that I have to stay warm until the rain stops."

"Miss Katie, I have an idea. I'm going talk to my parents and see if you could stay in our guesthouse until you can get your own place again," said Little B.

"You will do that for me?" exclaimed the little old lady.

"Yes, I will."

"Bless your little hearts..." She smiled as she put her food and new clothes in the shopping cart.

"Well, we have to go Miss Katie." Little B said, noticing his watch. "We have to be home before dark. We will try to come by tomorrow."

They said goodbye and Little B and his friends ran home. Little B's Mom and Dad were sitting on the couch watching TV when he walked in the house.

Joining them on the couch and sitting in between the both of them, he took a deep breath for the second time that day. "Mom, Dad...I have to ask you both a very important question...

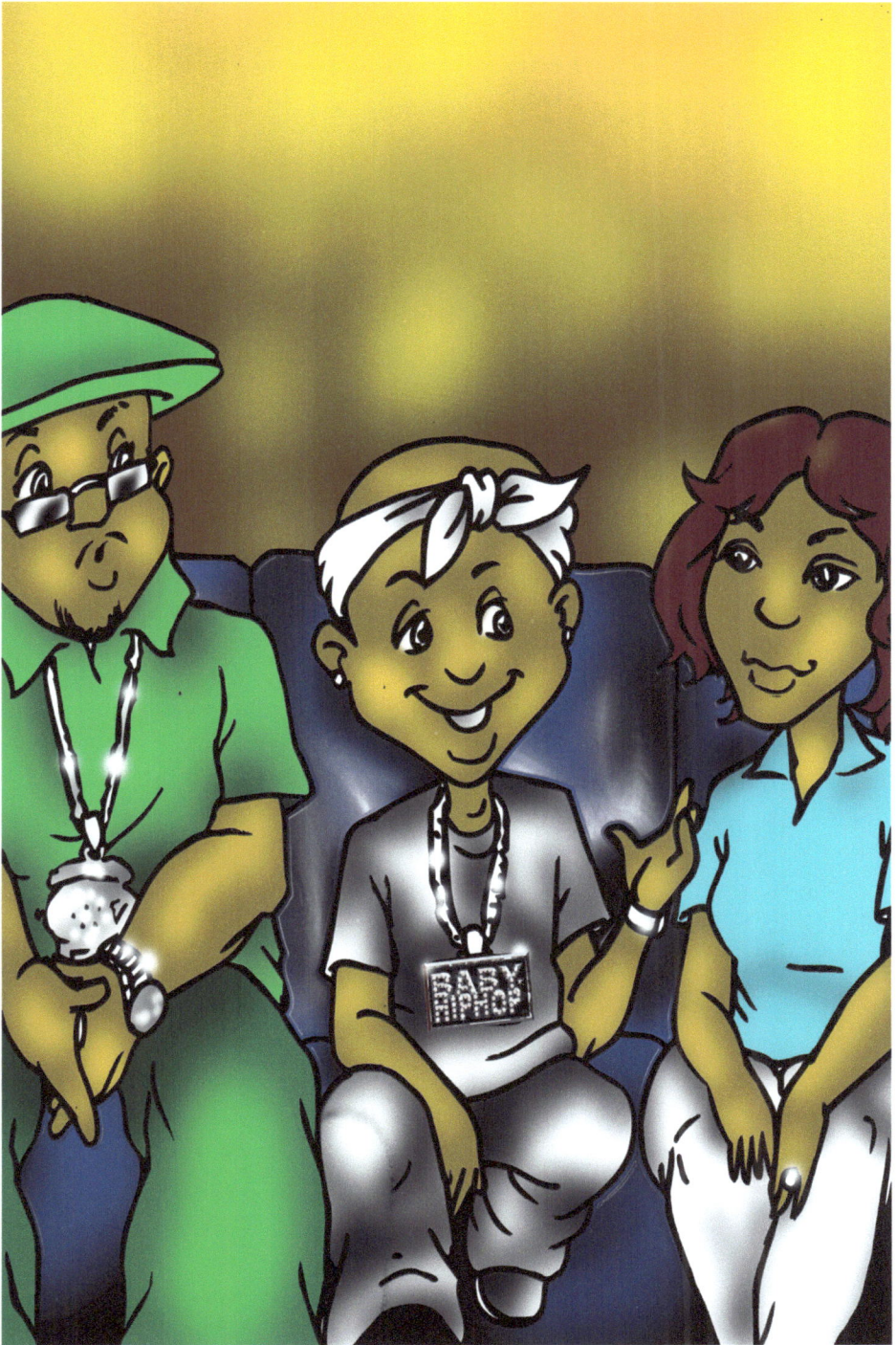

...Mom, do you remember when I asked you for some old clothes yesterday? And when you two were talking at dinner and I asked for seconds?"

Mrs Hip Hop nodded, "I did notice you ate a little more than usual. What about it?"

"I didn't eat all of that food. I gave it to someone who really needed something to eat and some clothes to wear."

"Who did you give it to?"

"Well Mom, I know you and Dad told me not to talk to strangers but this stranger really needed our help."

"Who is it, son?" asked Mr. Hip Hop. "She's a homeless old lady, Dad. Me and the boys were headed to the park yesterday and we saw this little old lady eating out of a garbage can. We felt very sorry for her so we offered her some candy that we had in our pockets. Then we talked to her for a while and she said that she lost her house in a storm and she'd been living on the streets ever since."

"You know I don't like you talking to strangers." Mr. Hip Hop said firmly.

"But Dad, she really needed our help and plus she is old. You always taught me to be kind to people and so I was being kind." Little B explained.

"Okay. I'm not going to put you on restriction but you can't talk to every stranger that needs help; it's just too dangerous now-a-days." His father warned.

Mr. Hip Hop took a minute to think then finally he smiled and said, "Look, you're my son and I love you very much so I'll tell you what: we'll go talk to the old lady tomorrow when I get off work."

"Thanks, Dad!" Little B exclaimed, jumping up to hug his parents with joy. The next day, Little B took his parents to meet Miss Katie. She was sitting on the same bench she had been sitting on the day before. Little B and his father sat down and had a conversation with Miss Katie.

Mr. Hip Hop said, "Miss Katie, my son told me all about your problems and I'm sorry you've had to experience such a horrible ordeal. I can't find myself just allowing you to sleep out here on the streets like this knowing how much my son cares about your well being.

We really don't feel that this is a thing to ignore so we would like to make you an offer. Little B, do you want to be the one to ask her?"

Little B grinned and nodded to his father. He turned to the old lady and asked sincerely, "Miss Katie, would you like to let us take care of you until we can find your daughter?" Miss Katie looked both happy and surprised as she began to cry.

"God bless you and thank you very much! If there is work that I can do to repay your good will, I'll do it."

"Don't worry; we need to take care of you first." Said Little B with a glowing smile.

They helped her gather her things out of the shopping cart and placed her few possessions in the trunk of the car.

The Hip Hop family took Miss Katie to her new home and that night, Miss Hip Hop prepared a big dinner to welcome her.

There, the little old lady happily stayed with the family and helped to take care of them as the family continued to grow for years and years to come.

The End

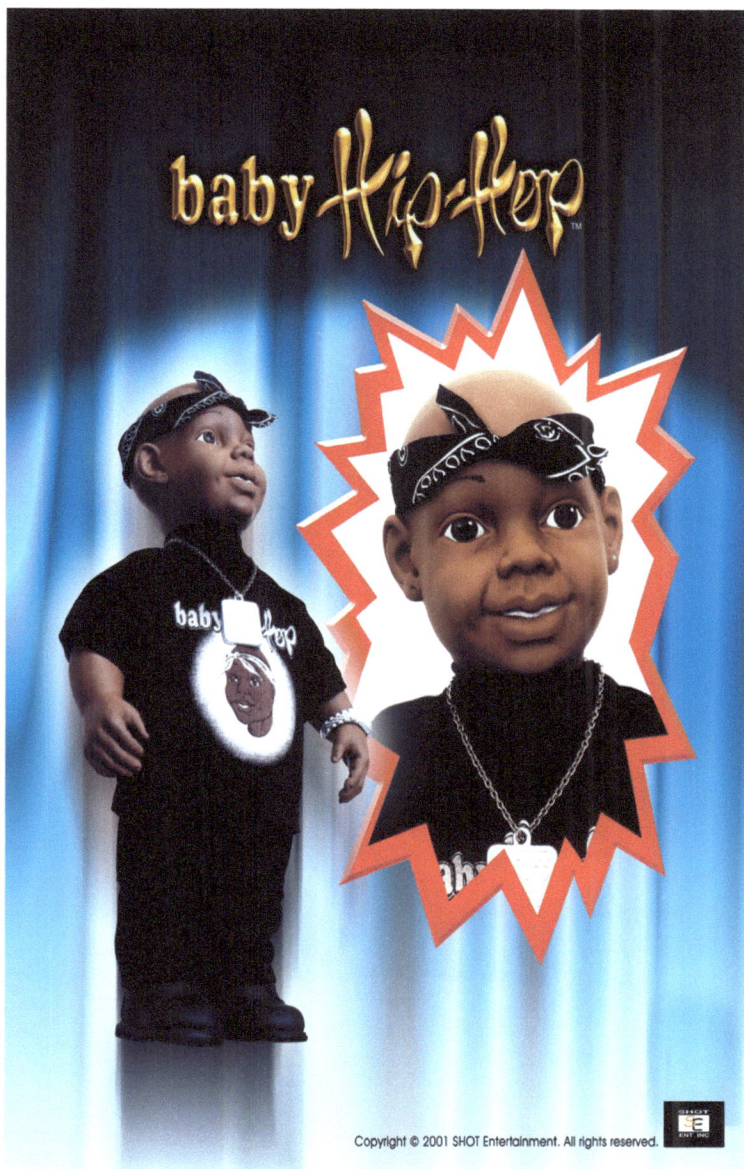

Baby Hip -Hop Rap & Count
Educational CD Now Available On ITunes

Baby Hip Hop Bio

Baby Hip-Hop was invented in 2001 by a well known rap artist by the name of D-Shot he is the brother of rap mogul E-40. D-shot's main goal was to provide a positive music related learning product for average and below average learning kids who enjoy and relate to Hip- Hop music. D-Shot's objective is to capture the kids who can rap and sing a full Hip Hop song before they can learn how to count to twenty or learn their ABC's. By years of observation D-Shot has learned by watching and observing his own to kids, I didn't realize how powerful music was until my own son started having problems learning his states and capitals so I invited my son to the studio and made him a song called Fifty States. The results of the song were tremendous it improved his ability to learn his States faster and easier by raping and singing the song. The whole purpose of this method is to go after the kid's interests and supply them with the education tools within their interest.

Baby Hip-Hop is the world's first educational rap star who helps other kids solve everyday problems threw rap music. What is so unique about Baby Hip-Hop is his ability to teach kids how to rap, count by lessening to good quality educational music. As you can see this isn't just any ordinary intellectual property this is a rap star which represents the Hip Hop music culture for children between the ages of 3 to 12. Baby Hip-Hop is a 3-year-old black Afro-American rapper he is Baby Hip Hop.

40